LIGHT EVERYWHERE

CEES NOOTEBOOM

LIGHT EVERYWHERE ⋮ selected poems

Translated by David Colmer

LONDON NEW YORK CALCUTTA

N ederlands
letterenfonds
dutch foundation
for literature

The publisher gratefully acknowledges the financial support of the
Dutch Foundation for Literature for this publication

Seagull Books, 2024

Original poems © Cees Nooteboom, 1960, 1964, 1970, 1978, 1982,
1989, 1999, 2000, 2012

First published in English translation by Seagull Books, 2014

English translation © David Colmer, 2014

ISBN 978 1 8030 9 446 5

British Library Cataloguing-in-Publication Data
A catalogue record for this book is available from the British Library

Typeset by Seagull Books, Calcutta, India

Printed and bound by Hyam Enterprises, Calcutta, India

CONTENTS

Light Everywhere (2012)

LIGHT EVERYWHERE

ENCOUNTERS

Light Everywhere ⋮ 2012

lifelines

And that afternoon they left the world behind.
Spinifex on the roadside, animals with names like flowers.
The sun was someone driving towards them,
only at dusk did their will diminish,
the road slinking out of the mirror, a sense of completion.

Now they would find somewhere to sleep,
arranging their naked bodies
in a place with nothing to go by.
Everything of their own invention, as lonely
as a beginning, a conversation
in an as yet non-existent language.

Filling a room with their presence,
gestures, voices, questions.
As if seeing an angel for the first time
and knowing he doesn't exist,
his wings tattered, dusty and mouldy,
his feathers too old to take wing.

That was what it was like when night fell,
the angel combed his hair,
arranged the wings he couldn't
remove and slept
in the only bed.

evening

In memory of Hugo Claus

The blue chair on the terrace, coffee, evening,
the euphorbia reaching for absent gods,
full of longing for the coast, everything
an alphabet of secret desires, the last
he sees before the gloom,

the mist in his head. He knows
the shapes of words will disappear,
only dregs in his cup,
the lines disconnected

that once were thoughts,
never again a word
of truth. Dismantled grammar,
blurred pictures without a bridge,

from the wind the sound
but no longer the name,
someone said it would be so
and death was on the table,

a slow servant, waiting
in the hall, smiling stupidly,
leafing through his newspaper
of senseless items.

He knows all this, the euphorbia,
the blue chair, the coffee on the terrace,
the day that folds around him slowly
and then swims off,
a gentle beast

with its prey.

the figure

The flower of the hibiscus lasts a day,
star of ephemeral fire, contradiction
of garden and sky, the man inside,
a body that resists, like every flower.

What he doesn't know: how true this is.
Is that figure real,
sitting outside in the stars' last glow,
not seeing the flower, burning itself
on the cold light of time-bound
morning, gathering flowers
from the dark earth and yielding to the violence
of sunlight?

The sense of grief now rampant within him
is in memory of a friend, a friendship
that is dwarfed
by so much decay.

What's sitting there now, a man or a poem?

The postman rides to the gate in his yellow shirt,
relates the world, hands over his letter
to a living being, never suspecting grief or this soul.
He sees the red flowers on the ground,
says it will be hot today,
and disappears into the light

and these lines.

trixy

Desolate species, humans.
Everything needs to be conquered,
a thousand Buddhas can't reverse the stream,
the stone in the middle remains unpolished.

The teachings of the titmouse.
What's that supposed to mean?
Minus ten and it's been working all day,
searching the hedge for a morsel.

In the distance I see the world,
in the corner, behind that car,
deeply passionate music
sweeps the litter into a heap.

It's here alone or more.
Woe to those who have the most words.
They're up to their knees in night,
their book of faces full of names
and mould.

In the stable thirteen goats are born.
Trixy barks at a shadow of white.

penobscot

Grey, however remembered,
the yacht, the angry yachtsman,
the admiral's house, the colour of vanilla,
tomatoes that needed bottling,
mint julep, living in a fragmentary
once.

Storms, the poet next door,
a seaman without a sea but with nautical rhymes,
an old country with French names, trees bent
under northern knowledge, memory, Indians,
trappers, words salvaged
from antique bordellos.

Growing old is lethal. Once again:
the autumn that precedes snow,
the painting without colours,
the poem without rhyme, that golden egg
disappearing in the goose
without a trace,

an aria of ice and hail,
heavens of extreme cold,
stories imagined and rejected
in which the yachtsman drowns
in a remembered winter
and exists as a poem,

but the last thought is of
her, the woman who disappeared,

who everything was about, the yachtsman, the bay,
the poet. The air it all breathed
is the loftiest fabrication, a life
possible now it's no longer

possible.

exile

The dock, the ship sailing away
over liquid glass.

Now I am alone with Chong Er,
my view, the plain,
my friends, the hermits in the hills,
turned almost to stone.
I will remain dark from now on,
far from the white deer
on which we rode in fields of cloud
and mist.

Between this and death,
a time for thoughts no one has written,
white-chalked shame on a slate,
my name liberated
from its letters, hollow
as a sound.

Ivory and jewels,
all things I knew, my shadow
disappears in a fold of time,
I pass on nothing, worn down
by the grit of every day,
I share the fate of stones and shells,

a prince without words
in a web
spun of nothing.

night

At night, past buildings of cloud,
and a last cafe of moonlight,
the dream of forbidden travels,
a gate, always closed,
now half open, the danger of a different
life, a poem

of an inverted existence,
in which death has no scythe,
but comes as a lover on hasty hooves,
caressing your breasts
and rolling out a carpet of stars
for you to lie on,

light everywhere, glinting
on the predatory teeth, the murderer's
nails and the gleaming knife
that writes the final word,
fire, and then your nobody's eyes
seeing endlessly for ever,

seeing who you were.

it

One poem ate the other.
Now a choir is singing and slowly approaching.
How many forms has invention taken?
Who, being absent, is standing by the garden hedge?

Take the slope, the wooded slope,
You know the back path and where to find the grit bin.
Near the tracks of the big tractor,
the fox lives with his religion.

See everything, understand nothing, the painter's motto.
Incomprehensible trees, misunderstood slope.
The fox nails his theses to the gate.
It is quiet in the mist.

The seventh thesis is about the miracle
and the fall. Count the stars. Give time
back to the man with the post. Ask the fox
what it is and why.

kozan-ji, myoe meditating

When I have disappeared
you will still sit there,
small mouth closed,
closed eyes full of celestial emptiness,
your sandals under the tree.

Are you thinking about something
or nothing, your very thin
hands folded together,
your body hidden
in the black
of your robes.

The cord for your prayers,
the small tub for the incense
dangling from a branch beside you,
you don't need them,
you yourself are the prayer.

Every time I see you,
a second has passed.
It's been like that for centuries, you
turn years into time.
The same two birds,
too far to identify,
the gently swaying trees,
you've grown ever quieter,

wind, rain and snow
have passed over the hills

with you there and elsewhere.
Nothing can touch you,
so lost before my eyes
that I can hear myself
fade.

april auf dem lande

It was summer and winter.
The water by the river,
how it rose.
Mist between the hills.
In the valley the expensive villas,
shuttered, white and pink.
Fox and owl
hidden out of sight,
a workday for herons and mice.
And the man who loved women, lonely,
not thinking about the birds.
Dew or rain
on the serrated leaves,
the call of a train
from the depths.
How many, he thought,
how many spokes in the wheel
of a single
day?

the candle

Him in his sailor's suit with the long,
broken candle. His white socks,
his mother's white shoes,
the loop of his shoelace. Below it,

ground, earth, the floor, the same as always.
On it, under it. White gloves,
torches and the other shoes,
shining black, in mourning.

Unforgettable, the break in the candle,
the snapped white wax dangling from the wick,
fate, valid even now. Her hand,
her gold bracelet.

His sailor's collar, blue, in the photo,
black against the white of her coat.
Her hand on his, her face,
his other face, invisibly remembered.

God, what tiny shoes!
Never stopped walking.

purgatory

Orbits, planets in a rusty glow, scorching,
late light over his town. The carmine-clad master
among domes and steeples, his book with that first line
look! in his hand. On the left, as big as a hemisphere,
vagevuur, a word from the north,

his other hand like a Buddhist mudra,
acceptance, tranquillity, subjugating evil,
behind him the mountain of slow penance,
waiting for light.

No wind, no movement, this place is subject to the laws
of punitive inertia, the folds of his cloak
vertical, no rustling in the laurels
on his brow, everything as strict

as a constant three lines, wave after wave,
the jagged layers full of sinners
passing the angel with the sword.

You could forget that they were the dead
and he the living one who had to write it down,
destruction, delight, fire,
heavenly joy in the foliage
above the flames,

vision without damnation.

without an image

Without an image a poem appears,
form emerging from the domain
of words, inherited
from people I never knew.

Language, polished in dreams, on pulpits,
moulded in beds and lonely rooms
for use in life and death, a weapon
in the struggle against chance, the tricks
of fate.

Who we were, our passage
through the enigma,
is written in words,
script as a daughter of speech,
whispering, lamentation, the marrow
of thought,

a testament to vanished
emotions, the tone of decrees for later
when the mob has dispersed,
departed for their speechless
homes.

riso amaro

Like nuns in a field of rice,
I read in Zagajewski,
and suddenly it's there, a map,
an atlas without names,
continents with unfamiliar
shapes, regions coloured green
between anonymous seas,

and immediately a picture next to it,
like in a modern schoolbook:
a paddy field in an unnamed country,
nuns up to their knees in water,
sweating in the sun,

heroines of agriculture,
reflected between the plants.
Veils piled on the grass.

Everything made of words is real,
even the rice tastes holy here,
you can eat it with chopsticks:

each grain
a word.

horace to pollio in 2005

Blunders, treacherous friends, suddenly you're
walking on a fire hidden under caustic
ash. Betrayal, the wheel of fate.
You are at a loss, you write
what they want to hear, you scorch your feet
but burn your soul.

No matter how many stories there are,
there is only one history,
unknowable, unrecognizable
to victims and villains.
Writing is patient, no matter whose it is.
Suffering has no number.

You write. The images of death and persecution
are ours. They weren't even people.
They don't keep you awake.
You suck the goodness out of the future,
where we no longer exist.

Your empty soul gave birth to a war,
scarecrows dancing on the table.
The provinces humiliated the Euphrates.
Quae caret ora cruore nostro?

Horace knew: every coast in the world
is coloured by our blood, a story
that ends in words.

But don't bother looking for us.

glove, year, photo

A hundred pictures, addicted to them.
A white glove, lace, like the cuff.
Thumb and index finger spread, behind them the eyes,
full of black seduction.

A woman I have never known.
The look in her eyes is unfamiliar, we are
an impossibility. Some year or other, eyes,
glove, hat, this is for ever.

Even her shadow has disappeared,
but not in this picture. I ponder your year,
your then and the rest of your life, those who
exclude me are the enemy,

between here and there,
the mutiny of desire,
up against the wall of time,
the laws of never again.

outside

I am not going outside,
I am outside. Midway between the palm
and the fig. Under the half
moon, seven hours to dewfall.
Droplets on the leadwort.

What do you call each hour
of the night, each minute
of the hour? If days have names,
why not minutes?

Each moment of our lives
should have a name
that is nothing like ours,
that has forgotten us. Each second,
a number in a log

of glimpses, overheard
mumbling, lines of poetry
alternating with headlines,
whisperings of snow and frost,
the slowest poem
of duration.

Everything a circle,
as round as a square,

everything for ever
wedded to itself.

recognition

Then he saw
in the park in Charlottenburg
a shadow silhouetted against the sun
surrounded by light
that blinded him.

Eyes meeting.
Hers, shy,
in keeping with the falling leaves,
the black of the pond,
the chill of another life.

What she saw?
A man on a bench
dreaming of a poem.

Autumn, late afternoon.
The ravens coming home,
raucous smudges.

utopia triumphans

Was it in these tones, spun
from golden voices, the high notes
of the women, the men below them,
behind them, a web of soaring
holiness, polyphonic longing
for light?

What could that country look like,
the place those mouths sang of,
hills in silvery light,
water that can carry feet,
translucent alabaster afloat
in clouds of ivory?

The godhead, which still existed then,
sufficient to itself forever, full
without us and permeating everything,
a golden fleece around creation,
surrounding each body with fire

now extinguished.
The voices move, the man
alone in his room drinks
from his different world, antiphony
of heavenly exile,
meant to live without
and outside his time.
Still allowed to hear the voices
through the punishments of war
and pain.

He hears memories
of other times, the triumph
of what no longer exists,
even now their sacred knowledge
a consolation for calamity and shame,

the clear and shining light
that illuminates his shadow.

landscape

So who is the one who,
at the end of the evening,
opens memory, unveils eyes,
sets down the landscape, the house across the way,
mirror image of this house
in which I live as my shadow?

The forest climbing the hills,
mist over the churning stream.
Why now?
In the snow, the tracks of deer,
in the distance, the mountains.
Why here?

Tumult fills the sky, the two cypresses
next to the statue of the dead man
stand motionless in the rain, the asphalt gleams.
This is where I am, my time
following behind me, an eternal footstep
of words,

I know who I was.

raison d'etre

We measure the moment, having left
the ancient town, last glimpse of the ramparts,
the town wall, the kitchen garden at the foot
of the graveyard, the mist veiling the rhubarb
and the dead.

No one knows us here, beyond an
ancestor, sheriff, deacon, church dignitary,
powdered wig. He recognizes our name,
but not me, a ghost from a future

of disenchanted days. Himself a beloved skeleton
in a bed of musty stone; me, a
soulless machine, a low negation
of everything he lived for.

Descendant and ancestor, the story
of a forefatherland. We kiss the ground that gave us
birth, betrays and awaits us. A flag that
constantly changes languages,
a soul in transit.

We wear away in a future someone else
and persevere. You were here
to exist without equal, and so too
will you disappear, a sigh in the book

of the state, a compatriot, a subject,
someone, a number in a hundred registries,
a faithful fiction of me.

a trail in white sand

Those we are not
those we ourselves are.

Those above words
those in words.

Those beside the idea
those that are the idea.

Who lays the trail
in the white sand
of the page?

Who explains it?

From the melting silence
the first sound

in the outermost cloister
the birds

in the innermost walls
the voices

morning responsories
matins and lauds

the cautious step
of hare

the flight of magpies
crows, buzzards,

nothing makes noise
until you add it up

Upanishad in the woods
of Bentlage

utterances without audible
voices

relating
their deepest truth.

This is so little
the inattentive

will not have
seen it

how columbine moves
how the new leaves

on the oak
quiver and waver

above the frivolous
flowers

antiphony, psalm,
gradual

around the old
night song

of male voices
now gone,

yet never
unsung

undone.

Past voices
make no sound

the text is left,
the teachings

of slowness,
the word.

Hare flattens its ears
against its neck

fear
of my steps

three storks
in the cloister meadow

hieroglyphs
drawn in the field

birds like sons
of pharaoh

thinking my eye
in search of a frog

their dagger thrust
a spark in time

The great arsenal
of ferns

the muffled yet
of moss.

The sayings sit
at the feet

of the sleeping master
and announce

the very public secret.

Is the spider
the start

or the end?
The sum

or the question?
Its many angled

web
writes a geometry

across the path,
the death

of the fly.
The spider spins

death
from its body

the fly
follows the track

in the strangling
maze

Euclidean
lines

pure
as church music

the logic
of sacrifice

and murder.
Bentlage

April
eleven degrees

rain over
the beeches

a scratch in the grey
of the pond

the soul,
says the Upanishad,

is a flame
the size

of a thumb.
Today

that's right.
The leaden

clouds
extinguish

the flame
of the sun,

the verse
says

the final
thought

repeating the gesture
of the circle:

those we are not
those we ourselves are

those above words
those in words

those beside the idea
those that are the idea.

Who draws the trail
in the white sand?

Who explains it?

juarroz

Hay ángulos que no pueden cerrarse

Corners that can't be closed, you say,
and how love knows them
and always goes back to them
like thoughts and words,
the paragraphs of the wind.

I consider those words,
and see you before me, small, smart,
in a blue suit,
an Argentinian gentleman
who wrote vertical poems
and felt at home in the geometry
of his own design,
though no instruments
could measure it.

You lived in a miraculous
continent of the mind
where our laws do not apply
and questions rule the roost
with the power of axioms.

A blue suit, a tie,
an aberrant arrangement of space:
access to that other
existent world,

poetry.

wittgenstein

Mein *Leben* besteht darin, daß ich mich mit manchen
zufrieden geben, Note 344, *Über Gewißheit*

Yes, but,
looking at your photo,
head half turned, hair pulled straight,
hiker in mountains, Austrian village school,
harried look, eyes showing a lot of white,
reality, whatever that is,
always up in the intangible air,
uncertain whether your hand is your hand, 456,
or what you can rely on, 508,
I, man of little faith, understand
why in that one sentence, 344,
life is the only word italicized.
We are satisfied that the earth is round, 299,
but what kind of sentence is
Nothing in the world . . . 384?
Questioning and thinking, thinking and questioning,
number after number, *Here I am*
inclined to fight windmills,
because I cannot yet say
the thing I really want to say, Note 400,
from the memorial of a knight errant
in a pitfall of his own design,
hunting between speech and knowledge,
still far from home.

hesiod

πίσσης τε δροφερης καὶ
κέδρου νηλέι καπνψ

Ancient poet, touched by the Muses themselves,
so you claimed at least,
with a branch of laurel,
or was that just boasting?

I stare at the fifteenth of your
fragments of unknown position:
'with the pitiless smoke of pitch
and cedarwood',
an uprooted line without a poem.

Kapnos, smoke, fumes, steam,
nèleès (poet.), without pity, merciless.
I sit with your written orphan on the table
while my neighbour burns off
brambles. I see the smoke
over the dry field, pitch black and menacing,
and smell that cedar,

a smell that's three thousand years old.
Was it a fire or a sacrifice,
or were you just watching your neighbour?
Hesiod, marble poet,
when will you finally
finish that
verse?

meng jiao

> Less than a day in paradise,
> and a thousand years have passed
> among men.

Fine, we believe everything in this
bitter legend. Two chess-playing boys
in painted mist,
the accelerated fall of time.

Wang Zhi, just his luck,
hiking through the mountains, high, cold,
in that same painted mist,
searching for wood for his fire.

Wang, silly Wang, why do you eat the date pit
they give you? Checkmate, the handle
of your axe rots away at your feet.
When you get home

you're a hundred years old. But the poem
remains, unbreakable lines
of spider web. Hats off, old cricket,
but why Wang Zhi?

The path in the Mountains of the Stone Bridge
is deserted, slowly the mist drifts
out of the painting, revealing (lower right)
a smudge of rust, the axe.

shelley

Stanzas Written in Dejection, near Naples

The waves are dancing fast and bright,
yes, and on the right the purple silhouette
of Capri, still, and the volcano on the left,
but quadrupled between them and here,
a road, and the temperature's reached forty.

The sea's a watercolour, true, I close
my eyes and see your early nineteenth century, but below
the suicidal traffic races by, a vicious world of greed
and pressing need, the nightmare you never saw.

The purple noon's transparent might
is darkened by an oily haze, only the beggars
are still the same, and the alienated angelus.
The City's voice itself is soft like Solitude,
and you were unhappy in your golden words,
capitalized sorrow. Forget it. Loneliness
today goes dressed in anonymity
and pop and ecstasy, but then a different kind,
and I envy you the strange, oh so
eloquent, flowing, rhyming, permissible complaining
that earned you immortality,
as long as it lasts.

We don't complain in verse but in infernal
images, in the Prozac of ringmasters
and psychics and all the things you couldn't
name yet knew while sitting here
and suffering between palms and rhymes and the despair
that was your fortune, and which sustains us still,
or now no longer.

borges

A una moneda

Rio de la Plata, the storm thrashes
the water. You who can still see
write the disappearing city in the name
of her letters, the mouth of the river,
the ocean. The poet's winter voyage.

But what's got into you?
Which of all your souls
now takes that coin from your pocket
and throws it from the highest deck,
a flash of light
in the black of the waves.

Or wasn't it you, but once again
that other one who's also called Borges,
the reflected man in the dreamt
poem?

Twice, you say, you have added something
to the history of the planet,
two ongoing progressions, parallel,
infinite perhaps,
your existence and that paltry coin's,
which there in the deepest depths now
embarks on the magic stages
of decay,
but doesn't know it.

You do, that's why you're jealous
and happy. Your secret pleasure

was seeing through fate. Eternal return,
infinity, imaginings to play with.

That's how you threw your work
into time,
words, begun as nothing,
as thought, sentences, poems,
writing transformed into a book
of marble, and then, drifting
and sinking, corroded
by thousands of unborn eyes,
back to words without a poet,
and further still,
stone letters slowly illegible,
whispering fragments,
the mysterious echo
of a prehistoric era,

until that one last
salvation,

absence
achieved.

descartes

Manus vero has ipsas

Philosophers have a thing about their hands
despite always writing with them,
or perhaps
that's why.

Wittgenstein was uncertain whether his hand
was his hand, *Über Gewißheit*, 456,
and Descartes, in his first meditation,
bending over the page, by the fire,
in the dressing gown that was not subject to question,
candlelit, *withdrawn in solitude*,
begins stone by stone on *the complete dismantlement*
of all he had thought until then.
And these very hands and this whole body,
my body, what reason could I have
to deny them? It is in full consciousness
that I move this hand and feel . . .

Vraiment? Or not? he asks afterwards,
but his question mark is a feint,
knowledge disguised as doubt, a one-man dance
of the mind in the theatre of Ergo Sum.
He knew the answer and only had to write it down:
in his Latin like cool clear water,
his French like polished glass.

But downstairs in the dark cellar,
the rodent Ludwig gnaws away
at the edifice of ALL THAT'S RIGHT.

virgil, fifth eclogue

aspice, ut antrum
silvestris raris sparsit
labrusca racemis

See how the wild grapevine covers the mouth of the cave
with its shoots . . .
Exactly, Mopsus, safely dead
in your fifth eclogue,
at that peculiar song festival for poetic shepherds,
you have a point.

Here too, against this wall of piled stone,
my grapevine grows wild. Nine months
since I've been here, flying from airport
to airport, a hasty moth
to neon. All that time, my vine
gripped the wall tight with the love
of plants for stone, waiting
for rain and light.

Let Menalcas yodel away
with his classical chatter,
forget your sorrow for Daphnis
and how to make it resound.
Enigmatic, this man who wrote you
in a capriccio of rustic, light-footed
sorrow: isn't he the same one Broch
has die so tragically to music
by Bruckner, accompanying his
millenium-younger colleague
on his descent into a hell of

mud and mange, calamity,
ash, ice and blood?

Strange, the paths poets take: Aeneas has only just carried
his father out of the ruins of Troy when he sees
Carthage in flames, hears
Dido's bitter lamentations,
and *there's* idyllic pastoral verse
rippling past Marie Antoinette's
arbour in a wash
of pink.

Hopla!

ungaretti

Mi tengo a quest' albero mutilato

I found your poem,
bilingual, on the Mercat de Sant'Antoní
in Barcelona. Italian, Catalan.

Now I'm sitting here with three dictionaries
translating 'I Fiumi', 'The Rivers',
written in Cotici, 16 August 1916,
the forgotten war you could never
forget.

The monuments, bayonets, heroic faces
and grieving women have become melodramatic,
Somme, Sedan, Isonzo,
one's all for one's country,
the sorrow disappearing with the survivors.

Only you are left.
Not walking like in those old films,
with that humiliating shuffle, no,
you go to the river slowly
like a young soldier
and lie down in the water
as in a grave of water,
and sleep.

L'Isonzo scorrendo	*L'Isonzo fluint*
mi levigava	*m'esmerilava*
come un suo sasso	*com a còdol del seus*

The water from the river
flows round you,
kneading and caressing you,
polishing you like a pebble.

Then you stand up
and walk out of the frame
over the water
to kneel beside your soiled uniform
for the next shot
like a Bedouin,
and see, so you say, what you are,
an obedient fibre of the universe.

A naked man alone by fast-flowing
water, Apollinaire, Owen, Graves, Ungaretti,
poetry is never just
about that one
war.

wallace stevens

some things, niño,
some things are like this

1

Roucou, roucou, Don Don
tom-tom, c'est moi,
lobster Bombay with mango chutney,
hoyo, hoy
let me start like that,
with the most frivolous notes
in your slow Gradual
as thoughtful poet and cantor.

Deference is called for, I know,
before this mighty gentleman,
who transformed poetry from song
and lament
into superior fiction,
reality, seen by the poet
at the hour of his moment,
without myth or credo,
an anti-Vatican
with your titles as totems:
Notes towards a Supreme Fiction,
Meditation Celestial & Terrestrial,
The Ultimate Poem is Abstract.

2

For you, no dream between
poetry and reality,
you rejected the story
of the sun as a god
that eclipsed the sun itself,
that was just a seduction, fuss and bother,
abduction from this sole existence,
this one time, here, now,
on the coincidental planet.

You were heavy of body, heavy in your slow and driving
fluent verse, and yet,
hoyo, roucou, tom-tom
Canon Aspirin and Nanzia Nunzio
hoobla, hoobla, how
with your French frills
between the sections,
triangle of modest jubilation
around the continuous bass
of the meditative bumblebee.

Your law is marble:
your highest fabrication,
writ line by buzzing line
your *mundo* for you alone,
now ours,
reality, always dressed
in a different thought
and only whole as a poem.

3

Adieu, waving *adieu adieu*
to the one who doesn't exist,
adieu,
because it had to do without, always,
and clear
with the sharpest eye,
always.

All that you achieved
in your unshakeable palace of words
is valid still—
the axiom of the sun,
the dictates of the pear and the rock—
and must be repeated
because that was the lesson:
*It is possible, possible, possible. It must
be possible.*

If that's not assurance!

Adieu, adieu.

poem

Do you know what a
poem should look like?
Bottom, side, rear?
Numbers? Letters?
And which colour?

Should it be like waves,
and what kind of waves?
Sea, lake, river?
Should there be room for everyone
and what should it cost?

I have known poems
so old you had to
help them cross the road.
Others were blind,
but there were also women
in the bloom of youth,
with thoughts like suckling lambs
and lips of testament.

There are no rules,
said the Master, sometimes
they are like stocks and bonds, then
more like marzipan,
and he danced on the marble steps
of the mausoleum

the day before he died
of a poisoned
sonnet.

stolen poem
Frans Budé 60

To heavy shrubs at the bottom of the garden,
everything gaping as if under a strange control.

Summer scorched us, the water of the lake was
    warm and sweet,
an hour of torment and lamentation.

Fingernails grow with such self-assurance,
you too must live with what you know.

Me? But am I that same man who once lived here,
who returned here?

Of all these things only a little is left,
writing that withstands decay.

Sit still, and listen to the last of our sea sorrow,
with whom can I enjoy the smell that was left me?

It all springs from this:
in an insignificant place

a shadow
under a stone.

Be, you.

poet

H. C. ten Berge 70

First name, last name, body,
that's what he clings to, mind, soul, person,
the always incalculable core
of creator and perpetrator
in a passing life,
fluid, polymorphous,

butterfly and falcon, speech
and objection, thoughts
spoken, but rather written,
life flowing like a river, deer
and ducks on the banks,
never alone,

in the distance churches, castles,
a prison, a monastery,
potentia maxima,
casino and confessional,
in this labyrinth
of all things possible, the poet moves
between share indexes and ditches,
his local, no-man's-land,
trying the dice
between the walls of fate,

the one or the six, honey or ash,
parlando or aria,
trying, stone or water,
win or lose, thistles or lilies,

with the horizon ever closer,
a life

full of hymns
that still
doesn't taste
like the sum.

poste restante

Oh, it's all so fine,
the way you write your poems,
eloquent parlando,
and you, thoughtful,
con moto,
and you, your tortured grammar,
rhymed and ragged,
a cry in the night.
Except today I have to do it differently,
without all too many words,
like the moon shining through
the mosquito net, here,
on my bed,
that simple,
that quiet.

Bittersweet ⋮ 2000

bittersweet

Bittersweet,
solanum dulcamara,
arrowhead leaves,
yellow stamens, the toothed
trap of dreams.

Bittersweet,
growing on fences and slag heaps,
serrated dagger in the dark,
secret betrayal
with a kiss.

Bittersweet,
the gait of the lover
in the house where cancer
has sat down with a knife and fork
to eat into my friend,

bittersweet,
those years of lust,
the moss on the stone
over no one,
his mouldy name.

Bittersweet,
this life of ours,
unequalled, floating through time,
and never looking back
at the door.

picasso, late etchings

In this cloud they couple,
in this black cloud, their ink-black lust
vented in copper, sharp and tense,
by the voyeur behind the curtain, he wants,

he wants this woman too and the man,
the double figure in which he
turns in on himself, curling up
like before, a century ago.

In that scratched embrace
he seeks a sea and a bed, screaming
for lost tides, eternal intercourse,
as homesick as someone
who cannot turn away.

spring

Something's eating the earth from inside,
something's digging, knocking, willing, growing
against the closed door of the ground.

They are ghosts,
with hats of flowers,
coats of fruit and butterflies.

Their domain is the undermost world,
their absence precedes their future,
soon they will come to haunt the daylight

with the boisterous beauty of summer
on the soil that's finally turned.

amsterdam, 1200

Between sea and sea,
salt marshes
behind dykes of seaweed.

Waterfolk, land makers,
black angels,
forefathers, gliding over mud flats.

They are the first,
dreaming walls of driftwood
in the wandering river.

Ame, water.
Stelle, safe place.

The name of their liquid
city.

paula modersohn-becker, still life, 1905

Porridge in a blue bowl,
bread beside it, half a loaf.
An egg, a lump of cheese,
flowers, tablecloth.

No time with these images,
it wasn't present.
The porridge an inedible brushstroke,
what does it all mean?

Art, how ravenously
you embrace the being of things!
I'd choke on that egg,
nobody eats the bread on that table,
and yet,
in the studio of my eyes
the paint now changes to food,
a still life with a man from the future,
a meal that keeps waiting for ever
for my then-so-invisible mouth,

my eternal hunger stilled.

fairy tale

Outside the bricklayer,
inside the mother.

The house that arises
hides a birth.

Grammar, syntax,
the power of becoming.

What are you lacking?
asked the shepherd,

wandering flockless and alone
on the outskirts of town.

Who knows me?
wrote the stork

like a banner
around the cock on the steeple.

To each his place,
thought the rat,

intent on dreams
to warm its bones,

closing the circle
by biting its tail.

Unnamed was the afternoon
when all this happened.

Now they had to wait
for the end of the riddle,

happy ever after.
The first sense of the word.

the poet li ho finds an arrow
on the battlefield

Chang-ping. I'm following you there, with your two horses.
Why two? Powdered bone, grains of vermilion,
lacquer dust. You had those three in your very first line.
You have bronze flowering from a flood
of ancient blood. White feathers, a gilded shaft
wasted away in the icy rain, all you find is
a triangular wolf's tooth, broken, a barb, an arrow.

The bookkeeper of mortality. That was you.
Dead in 712, that battle long past, the poet
alone on the deserted battlefield. Long wind, you say, short
daylight. Then stars, tears, an empty night. Your words.
I see you, wandering through the mud, still with those
    two horses,
searching for weapons, for rings, for bones,
between bushes and rocks. The black flag

of cloud over you. In the distance the inn
where messengers sleep on their way to the capital.
You rode east. You hear, and so I hear,
the screams of ghosts from the rotting bodies.
Mutton and curds, your only offering,
you ride in a a whirlwind, buds of fiery red
in the blasted reeds, the honking of geese,
that's how you find your weapon,
rusty brown, traces of blood, corroded bronze,
point jagged, broken, the barb that once pierced
a man. There you go, neglected poet,
a man with his trophy. In the East Quarter you ride to
    South Street.

You barter your find with a pedlar,
a broken arrowhead for a votive basket.
Was it worth the trouble? Yours? Mine?
I think so. A barb, a basket,
your poem in a language you never heard.

summer

Summer never runs short.
Plantains, white nettles, ground ivy, sweet william.

Mills turning in the swollen morning,
a cloud like an udder on the cow of the sky.

The river rolls itself up in the depths of day,
herons written in mirrors, enchanted thrushes

in the open palace of the trees,
balminess, excess, felonwood,

the cuckoo rhymes its call
to the book of the sun.

rilke, painted by paula modersohn-becker,
1906

So that's Rilke, in 1906,
face leprous with poetry,
eyes reduced to pupils, black marbles
on death's pavement.

Collar stiff and high, ears like an afterthought
with a spot in the middle
that hears what the world denies
before poetry begins.

This is no portrait of a body,
a requiem has been turned
inside out with a knife of sonnets,
beauty infected and burnt.

No princesses, no countesses here,
his haircut slices a square of horrors
from that forehead,

here, only the mouth of grief.

distortion

Never who you wanted to be,
who you thought you were.
The wrong costume
in a skewed world.

Always getting halfway with lies,
the oldest fiancé, never one to say
the homespun truths

are the deepest. For you,
appearances were closer
than the first principle,

too much world, too much moss
on your statue, holding the book
you didn't want to read,

a man of flesh turned to plaster,
an angel of shadow, alone,
cloaked in the empty profession
of your name.

the first photo of god

That's what I looked like after that first day.
Just me with my stones of stone.
Just me with my skies of sky.

That was the day I was still happy,
the earth still formless and void.
Only afterwards did I create the trees,
the animals, the army and that photographer.

I often think wistfully of the day
I made him as the first of all.
The two of us together in my creation,
me in my purple coat among my skies of sky,
him with his eye like a mirror
on my stones of stone,

and nothing else.

solanum dulcamara

Tapping and rustling, ghostly forms
at the night window, despicable
memories that were irresistible,
shock of poisonous velvet,
guilt, never to be undone,
ground crystal, vicious, always
the night side of beauty,

                         bittersweet.

And what did he get in return for his fears?
A few poems we are now reading,
frayed, painful sentences
that don't rhyme,
haunted by his ending.

His disease was nightshade, awake
when the world is weak with darkness,
when shapes are dangerous, when silence
has claws and the teeth of a bat,
longing for eternal sleep.

Bittersweet was the cup he drained,
calling out to the friends who had already left
with words that have to bear the burden
of continuing without him.

                     Bittersweet,
his poems as the secret of a life
that was reluctant to bear itself,
the gentle purple of its flowers,
the poison of its fruit.

autumn

This hunting scene folds in
now the slowest painter suggests it.

Mausoleum, organ music,
shields with deer and peacock.

No words, no rain,
no judgement,

the invented farewell
withdraws into itself,

an animal wanting to sleep
because it has heard the winter,

the tally-ho of sadness
on the edge of the afternoon,

the departure again and again
of every separate leaf.

noche transfigurada

On the terrace in the dark, your voice:
today, too, I didn't see anyone
stealing the heavenly fire,
the repository of light.

We were silent. The names of painters and poets
wrote their radiance in the gleam.
The night was a shadow
gathered from other shadows,

a game of double-crossing chess.
That was the reality, stuck
under the whip of the eternal charioteer.

Some think and suffer silently,
others tend a dream of cunning violence.

And on the last of days
nobody collects the names. Nobody sees
how the fire that had always fed him
slowly loses its leaves
and dies.

It Could Be Like That ⋮ 1999

self

And what if we leave our selves
behind?

There they go, no goodbyes,
pouting and brooding,
in search of something better.
Not even looking back.

And us?
We have to get used
to this radiant landscape
of past and future,

time, bright and shining,
without a now.

post

But how clear *are* your ideas?
the postman asked. In that instant
the sky darkened,
but that had nothing to do with it,
it's like that here,
from one moment to the next.

It's going to pour, he said, and so it did.
Big fat drops. I saw the bay behind him,
a plane labouring through the clouds,
heavy, landing.

What happens to seconds like these?
How much noise is superfluous?
Which conversations resist being
crushed against the wall of time
by a lack of memory, somewhere
at the back of a dream?

Fiction, a house on a hill,
the psalm of rain, page six,
postman, descent, the downhill path
to oblivion,
his, mine,
time's bacon.

Like someone turning a page
without having read,

everything written for nothing.

latin

In a dark forest, of course,
and years past the middle,
I wouldn't need to invent
a vernacular.

Nothing I had to say
would resound, my words
would have changed back
to Latin, illegible, closed.

Poet, clerk, secret deacon
of the smallest parish,
the sect of hidden meaning,
turned inward,

a gnosis of masked sentences
in an ever less recognizable script.

Eye Sight ⋮ 1989

bashō

1

Old man in the reeds the poet's mistrust.

He sets off on a trip to the North he writes a book
with his eyes.

He inscribes himself on the water he has lost his master.

Love alone in things cut out of wind and cloud.

This is his calling visiting friends to say goodbye.

Amassing lips and skulls under fluttering skies.

Always the kiss of the eye translated into the constraint
of words.

Seventeen the sacred number that will contain what
appears.

Past decay frozen to stone like a butterfly.

Polished fossils in a marble tide.

The poet passed this way on his trip to the North.

The poet passed this way once and for ever.

2

We know poetic poetry the vulgar dangers
Of moonstruck and serenade. Perfumed emptiness,
Unless you turn it into stones that shine and hurt.
You, old master, polished stones
That can bring down a thrush.
You carved the monument that bears your name out of
    the world.
Seventeen stones like arrows a school of dead singers.
See the poet's track at the waterside.
Headed for the snowy interior. See how the water
    erases it,
How the man with the hat writes it down again.
Preserving water and footsteps, setting past movement
    still,
So that what has disappeared still exists as something
    that has disappeared.

3

Nowhere in this universe have I a fixed abode,
Is what he wrote on his cypress hat. Death doffed his,
As well he should. The sentence remains.
Only in his poems could he live.
Soon now, you will see the cherry blossoms of Yoshino.
Put your sandals under the tree, lay your brushes aside.
Stand your stick up in your hat, recreate water in lines.
The light is yours and so is the night.
Soon, cypress hat, you too will see them,
The snows of Yoshino, the icecap of Sado,
The island that sails to Sorën over tombstone waves.

4

The poet is a mill that turns landscapes into words.
Yet he thinks like you and his eyes see the same things
The sun that perishes in the horse's mouth.
The outer shrine of Ise the beach of Narumi.
He hoists the sail of grief he sets course for his task.
His jaws grind flowers to make foot after foot of verse.
The accounting of the universe as it appears every day.
In the North he recognizes himself a pile of old clothes.
When he is where he will never be again you read his
    poems:
He peeled apples and cucumbers he painted his life
I too have been seduced by the wind that buoys the clouds.

lucretius

Housed in your body, one poet,
One thinker. The poem is a cosmos.
The world, a word.
Your thinking was chance
In verse with nothing left to chance.
Your letters, atoms.
Cicero was right, though he didn't know it.
The twenty-one letters of the alphabet
Still spell your name.

duality

A marriage of body and soul, the way each
Imposes constantly on the other,
Sorrow wearing the face of pain,
Illness masking itself with fears, the way wounds
Change thoughts, each accepting
The other's form, the death of one
Creeping into the other, the way each of these entangled
Twins always suffers along with the other
Until the body breaks like a vase and
The soul flows out like water.

And so you broke the vase you were
With the hand that wrote your book and
Your soul flowed away
To where I can read it.

fire

Leaden was the afternoon.
Hare slept, partridge dreamt
The death of the hunter and
Spider spun Euclid's nets.

And yet. Smouldering under the trees was the seed
Of the fire that leapt up,
Broke loose and raced around like
A rabid wolf, howling and
Snapping at nests and cobwebs.

Only ash was left and the wind,
When it came, hit the
Iron gleam in the charred trees,
Hurled its air into the
Silence, and

Gone was the flower of
Fire.

atoms

Remove the red of movement
From the timid square
Of your thoughts.
Watch as it falls in the empty stall
Of space with the drops of
Clear particles,
Always denied connection
To other things,
In the unthinkable dream of nothingness that exists
Without content.

He thinks this and composes his thoughts
As poetry until they are down and
Resound in the book of the sleeping
Universe.

mirror, reflect

The image you emit is so fast,
It doubles you:
A man of flesh sees
A man of bronze looking at him.

How thoroughly you are broken down
Until those invisible particles
Make you visible again
As a man who is also you,
And shares his name with you.

It means nothing, your not knowing
The timing of those images.
Your being and emitting them and
Capturing them again in the lakes of your eyes,
Your seeing this and saying so
In the hexametric surge of your words,

That was the miracle.

justice culinaire

This is what we have learnt:
The entrée under our ivory roof
Is home to many muses
Divided in equal portions of
Confusing love.
Two books that never read each other.

A cook wouldn't be fazed, soaking,
blanching. But they're self-willed.
Each half runs its own regime,
United only in the pan.

That didn't bother you,
Titus Lucretius Carus.
You served up art as knowledge,
Knowledge as art, a casserole of
Beauty and wisdom.

Cosmos, body, atoms, infinite space
Weighed and sautéed in hexameters like
Da Vinci dissecting a womb, like
Einstein playing the violin.

Y ya los batintines de tu léxico aturdían tus ojos

Guillermo Carnero, 'Variaciones y figuras sobre
un tema de La Bruyère', *Ensayo de una teoría de la
visión*

Se funden el sonido que de lo oscuro va subiendo hasta cortar la garganta, el cuerpo del que avanza por el templo contemplado por el silencio, sorbido por la claridad, el ojo que traspasa las ventanas, en un deseo insoportable de perderse en el ojo que a través de las ventanas le traspasa.

Serafin Senosiáin, 'Mallarmé', *El Espejo Invisible*

1

An exercise in orthodoxy

        against the deception

of seeing.

        The saint with the lion

and skull

        is no singer.

        He who doesn't break

his gaze

        sees nothing.

He who doesn't complete

        the observation

repeats

        what is seen,

laying an egg

        in the dove's nest,

like nature.

        I am not nature,

my battered scaffolding

        knows no laws

beyond those I have found.

2

I wanted to make
                    what no one has ever made,
a palace
                    of closed constructions
in their own
                    void.
My secret roads
                    led no further
than the farmer or hunter,
                    extensions
of field and prey. Each image
                    inherited
from images. All I do
                    is rearrange the hierarchy
according to a grim law,
                    my palace.
Paragraphs, appearing
                    in this order
for the first time,
                    an inescapable thought.

3

You would have preferred me
                    brighter,
like the world
                    I come from,
but that world
                    is black
like a shroud,
                    unforgiving
as stone.
                    That is my
heritage.
                    That is how I live
in my jerry-built
                    constructions,
with ashen
                    pennants and hatchets,
spatulas, lines,
                    tortured colours,
machines
                    that don't produce a thing
except
                    their essence,
illusions
                    of volume
and silence.

4

You call me
              your cherry-eyed
angel,
              you love it
when I dance,
              but I dance
like a bear
              on a chain
with my
              mild bowels
my square
              claws,
guillotines,
              swords,
retorts.
              My cage,
the preponderance
              of black,
the grey
              of polar grime,
boulders, the dead,
              the nail
through the heart
              of the lily.

5

They are monks
        in the service of my
monastery,
        never again
will the colours
        leave their posts.
        I am their
exhausting,
        murderous
angel
        with my single-
mouthed
        voices,
my prized
        violence.

6

Temptation,
              that's how you
operate,
              longing
for colour,
              I too
know those feelings,
              I feed them
sparingly,
              what there is
I've stolen
              from the brothel
of sheen,
              from fire
and dance.
              But my steel
is transparent
              because it wants
to think
              a thought
of ash.

7

All that
                    is study.
The endless
                    mist,
the breviary
                    of my thought
in the cell
                    of my eye.
You follow me
                    with a voice
I wasn't looking for,
                    that would risk
that same stringency,
                    the grieving
of the unmade
                    for its loneliness,
the discipline
                    of disintegrating
forms.
                    But you stayed
away from here
because it is cold
because I
                    bear
that cold.

what there was to see

A psalm for the art collectors,
written by the paintings.

1

The sight of us. Stay outside if it's too much
for you to bear. We transcend your temporal eye,
and, what's more, our language is not for seeing.
A dialect, if you like, oscillating between the concepts
aversion and distance.

We are fixed in place. The silence
between us is the silence of forms. No outdoor cafes,
no fluttering fans, no waiters or tips. An asphalt theatre
and we are the actors with voices of tar and metal.
The audience, a row of blind chairs.

That's how we see the dance that no one sees. A chisel
in the wall of light. A crowd of backs.
A bird in an empty cage. The shadow of that bird.

The doctrine of the violence things bring upon
        themselves,
the lessons of slowness and time.

2

You said,

       when we saw you, *and then?*
and then? A story was required, nothing
else would do.

           You don't hear our silence,
chattering on in your bankrupt voice
about your inner being, your convertible
melancholy, the sex of your money. Your bank
is always sealed, your shares
sleep under a bridge.

       You don't know that. You rejoice
with your tally-ho, your broiled wife,
your fried child,

           hunting horn, flute,
your honeyed trail over the registry.

       We went home,
where we already were. There was neither door
nor windows. Behind the walls we heard you
still buzzing about art intensifying life,
the sobbing
of your madrigal.

       Our clock
ticks just once a day.
       Only then were you quiet.

3

Our view: mist. But a mist made of slate.
Behind which no one risks their life.

We cannot be seen, but we are not invisible,
the dance of shadow in the always repeatable
cave. Perhaps a straw colour will please you,
a dead red, a shade of black. Your arrow
flies past but never strikes.

That's not because of us. We came out of a different
eye. That wrote us like a field in August,
scorched, burnt. Named, one of your memories.
Definitely not us.
Or a woman once seen at a wedding,
against the wall of a church. We know nothing
about that woman. Water in a creek, onyx, that which you
call black. It leaves us cold.

We are contained within our intentions, your eyes
are outside us, like Argus' before Hermes killed him.
He never found the way in. If we are anywhere at all,
it is in your furthest thoughts,
the ones you cannot reach.

While you look at us we slip away.

4

Someone considers us,
a mouse stares at a chandelier.
We allow it.

The powdered metaphysics
of those looks settles like condensation,
undrinkable.

Our slow and leaden champagne
under iron palms, granite petit fours,
this afternoon has already lasted a year.

Who paints, who drinks the river?
A year before the retreat inside.
The rustling of a single word.

the inner eye

1

The visible world channels the image
through the open eye. The inner eye

unfolds it, making it new again
in new light. Give them names.

Animals, squares seen in dreams,
halls and gardens

become images for the invisible
eye. This is how the soul colours

the eye with an eye to new images.
As strict as autonomy, an imperious

regime, far from similarity,
recognition, consolation. Dissected light,

degraded matter, visibility inverted,
unfaithful to its form,

each thing slipping from its word,
plummeting without a safety net.

Meaning shrugs off tradition,
demanding a new location,

but the word does not replace
an image with an image.

Sovereign in its own domain, it prescribes itself,
as yet unrecognizable,

a hand without numbers in an open clock,
captured by the eye

so that the viewer makes a vision
of the seen,

a world.

2

Shadow and light from a newfound land
order me in,

a hunter,
with his dog a third eye

that sees what was seen, how a view
became an insight and then the outlook

I now stare at, region, prey, lairs
and dens beyond me, an untraceable

trail, painted
on my inner skin,

the skin
of my internal man,

who drinks in the image,
as slow as nature, absorbing

it in his own tissues, place of abode, wellspring,
the house of his inner house,

one of many
in which we live as a species,

order of dreamers,
seers

of the dreams we are and seem to be,
who we are.

La letanía de Ibn Arabi en su carta mecana enmudece: Abd Allah b. al-Arabi 'entregóse con fervor al combate ascético viviendo en los desiertos'; Muhammad b. Asraf el de Ronda 'anduvo siempre vagabundo por los montes y lugares desiertos, apartado del mundo y sin acogerse jamás a lugar alguno habitado, durante cerca de treinta años'; Salih al-Jarraz 'se trasladó de Sevilla a los alrededores de Ronda, para vivir en el campo, en medio de la soledad y aislado de las gentes'; Abd-al-Sallam, 'el giróvago, andaba siempre peregrinando por las sierras, sin detenerse jamás de asiento en ningún lugar fijo'; Abu Yahya al-Sinhayi 'siempre andaba por las playas, prefiriendo los lugares desiertos y solitarios'; Ibn Arabi: 'Yo me aparté del mundo para vivir aislado en los cementerios'. La enumeración toma las ansias de soledad, las adensa, las vislumbra en el ojo hirviente del sufí. El hervor traslada el ojo del páramo a la luz, del yermo al calor, del silencio venteado en el que se oye a las piedras.

Serafin Senosiáin, 'Ibn Arabi', *El Espejo Invisible*

1

Blind man on a country road,
searching for his senses,
falling through the hatch
of light.
Unable to stay
where he had begun
to sing.
Other voices
had sung before him,
but he surpassed them
with the shuffling
of his feet,
his rhythm.

2

His humming was a repetition
of earlier mythologies,
not without necessity
or lust. The nights of the wanderer
are long. His thoughts turned to crystal
and cinnamon,
women, gestures,
the treacherous shadows
of words, the sand
between things
and words, a name
for himself.

3

His voice followed him
like a pet,
with echoes
of earlier choirs
and their celebrations,
the bacchanal of sight.
He painted mantras,
Chinese melodies, psalms,
antiphonies, thoughts
and analogies, hymns,
refrains, he hummed
softly without counting
his steps, a song
in service
of the eye.

4

Eye of the painter
who paints his self-portrait
as a repetition of eyes,
the square eye
of the Taoist sage
on a fleeting country road
like his,
skin full of Argus eyes
that can only look out,
the broken eye
of death,
the egg that drowned
in the Lethe
while you said your
evensong.

5

Evil eye
that kills without weapons,
the long eye of the hero
against blind desire,
the sightless eye of the seer
who announces fate,
vespers full of grim
spectres, responsory
of violence.

6

The eye that leaves the body
without ever leaving it,
the eye that could not see the sun
without becoming light itself,
iris, gazelle, shell
without equal,

in the wings of the evening
he continues to name
this constant
gazing,

target, bull,
the soft song of the hunter,

the litany of the eye.

the eye's sights

SILESIUS DREAMS

Dreams are true because they happen,
　　　　　untrue because no one sees them
except the lonely dreamer,
in his eyes they are his alone.

Nobody dreams us while we know it.
The heart of the dreamer keeps beating,
his eyes write his dream, he is separated
from the world, asleep inside and outside
of time.

The soul has two eyes, that's what he dreams.
One watches the hours, the other sees
through them
to where duration never ends,
where watching becomes seeing.

CAUDA

Look at things, see them exposed
in their metaphysical innocence
unsure of their existence.

Remember the conversation
in an arbour, a northern summer,
hydrangeas, an indisputable frog,
roses, masks.
Incense without a church.

A butterfly flapping its wings in China,
changes a gale in Finland.
Someone said so, you kept quiet,
already knowing.

When do paintings shrug off
the painter, when will this same material
become a new idea? The evening mist crept over
the lawn, drowning the avenue, the fountain,
the house.

Music, the splash of oars.
Someone turns on the light, someone
doesn't believe in dusk.
The unanswerable question drifts
past the window.

Paesaggi Narrati
(The Landscape
Tells the Story)

1982

empty quarter

The mountain slumbers underground,
And high above the sand that devours me
Hangs the seductive wing
Of a river as dead as the sun.
I was everywhere, a dog being chased
Through a world on its head,
With my tracks lost in a sandstorm
Like a word without letters,
Like a name without a soul.

altiplano

I am a messenger, racing
From forecourt to forecourt,
A nameless runner
With the king's word next to his heart.

In the dark, dogs bark.
In daylight, not a sound.
Agaves guard the distance, knives drawn,
The palace of hatred.

The toad's padded feet
The snake's deceitful writings
I recognize these riddles,
They are etched on my skin like a name:

One day you' ll be stuck here for good.

Bait | 1982

nerval

We stood on the square of reason and pure doubt
and saw his silk-laden ship
steer its lightless course to the ocean,
there to be lost.

On board, portraits of fathers on vases,
paintings of all our phantoms and doubles,
a rearing tomb of sonnets, the ghost writing of his
    thought,
everything we knew and dreamt
in the thorny cage of the storm.
lit by crystal lightning,
he disappeared from view.

Leaving us behind like a questioning statue,
turned to stone between laughter and reverie, children
    of the mire,
a shrinking sign still haunted by time,
the husk of a monument
whose origins have been forgotten by all.

elko, nevada

These gods were different,
resembling us,
and though they didn't have hearts,
they could move.
Sometimes they gave money.

Orpheus and Eurydice,
I saw them in this reflecting temple
of dancers and singers,
alone in the ash-violet glow,
dead, mauled and rotten,
dressed in nylon and madness.

Two blond, scorched heroes,
reverberant with fate,
emerged from under the world,
and me the masked writer.

It is nine o'clock in a time,
in some order or other.
Beyond the desert and mountains
the sound of their voices decays.

The young girls scream
at the man lost in thought,
covering the town
with their lust.

snow

As if it doesn't snow in *your* head!
As if *your* memory is different,
not like snow at all, not snowing
down on everything,
blurring everything.

A thought of us
descends over the once sunny landscape.
That double, gently rounded hill, over there,
in that curve near the palms,
that's our persons.

They're lying there comfortably on the beach.
Books of ice, cigarettes of snow,
two left-over tourists
tempted by iceland,
roasted in crystal light.

That's how we forget ourselves
and fall, white and silent,
over everything from the past,
we drift, floating and dancing,
over the white of what is gone.

bogotá

Three a.m.
I lug this cast-off life behind me
like a fisherman dragging his net along the shore,
heavy with water and dead fish
trailing their own blood.

Three a.m.
That's how I wake in foreign cities
to the sound of the cock being struck for the third time
for seeing a light in the darkness.
Sorrow doesn't shun me.
I ward it off with big words.

Three a.m.
Enormous crates of silence around my bed,
packed and sealed.
But the silence is thorny
and a source of pain that will not pass.
The silence smooths the path for the messenger's round
to say that morning brings night again.

And then,
I comb my bones, bundle them together,
fall in for another passage, step into the water
and live.

manáos

That it had to come to this:
me, on a bed in the tropics,
dreaming of an object I once gave you,
which still exists, perhaps, somewhere in the world.

It was a thing. It has its own life.
Without our names it will find its dealer
in a subsequent century. We, who wear down our lives,
imagine ourselves in a future of earlier years.
Impossible.

Now there are others. They know us less well,
they're not the same. And whichever dialect they use
to speak of lust or love, the simplest things elude them.
You never wanted to be grateful. You always liked to
     sleep in.
Your public side is in yellowing papers.

Trucks on red roads.
Ships with drunk Indians on the river as wide as a sea.
I read the letters in that childish hand
and dream of a thing I will never see again.

traveller

In the tortured reeds, those two women
wrapped in their cloaks.
They've been there for hundreds of years.
Tonight they guard my fear.

And you, the devil of my poisoned dreams,
pursuing and confusing me
on an Oriental evening like this,
what do you want?

There are so many things I haven't learnt,
I only know myself in reverse, a refugee
running to meet me,
fleeing punishment.

Two Japanese women, once seen
in a storm, preserved and drawn
in a flaming gust of leaves.

What are these things?

I am a traveller, who was looking for peace.

fin de saison

It ended up a month like October.
The colour of the wine was invisible,
the waiters drowned in the frozen
terrace.

This is how the demon did it:
he waded through the marble water
and lifted her shade from the rock.

It looked like this:
the wind blowing in over the sea
with the night in its wings.
The demon transported her shadow
to where I could never see it again.

That was how he put an end to the riddle she
had been. He burnt my eyes and ears
and smashed the past.

Then he released his prey,
broken and bled.
And me? Me, he left for dead,
with the last tip of the year.

cliff

I've hardly been here an hour
and yet you call me eternal.
Your centuries are my seconds.
While you think of me as hard,
I feel myself flow.
You are of flesh,
I am of stone.

We are both hidden in words,
but we designate the same thing.
Because you pass so quickly, I last so long,
but there is no difference.

And yet,
once there was no me
long before there was no you,
and one day I will disappear, crushed and pulverized,
just like you, unravelled, removed
without a trace.

My slow, ossified thoughts
know the same pride,
the same fall.

rock plant

Wherever you see me,
in whichever form,
an armour-plated animal,
a plant like a stone,
I am determination.

In the northernmost village on earth,
in a dead town's grave, in the unravelled fire
of deserts:
where no one can live, I exist
and I exist alone.

I make my food from grit,
water from marble, fire from ice,
tanned, scorched and tortured
on the world's barest shield,
I insist on life,

and I exist.

tree

Be me, become me,
just once in your restless life.
The wind that swirls round here
comes from two continents
to dance me like a man.

I don't have one,
I *am* my soul.
To speak my constant thought,
I rustle, wave and whisper,
the exemplary tree
with its language of just one word.

It's not the monks
who sing like humans,
but I who wait here for ever,
suffering the world's evil
in my unrepeatable,
guiltless shape.

scholasticism

This is the earth's most ancient dialogue:
the rhetoric of water
explodes on the dogma of stone.

But the invisible outcome
is known only to the poet.
He dips his pen in the rocks
and writes on a tablet
of foam.

fuji

1

Here, on the slow, grooved flanks,
the wooded, chestnut, so very snow-white slopes,
with the fine tracks of priests and poets,
radiant or dark in the surrounding world,
it floats or sails over swirling mists
like a shape beyond gravity,
like a mountain of light.

2

Here, fortified by walls of ice, seen
with a child's eye among bright blossom,
in the black bag of the night, reflected on water,
from a ship's dancing deck, on car and train windows,
it stands and watches among clouds and winds—
        visible, invisible—
drifts through the sky like a gliding bird
or weighs on the land like a state.

3

'Here,' the traveller can say a thousand times to that
    liquid vision,
'here,' the painter paints and drowns in his double
    landscape,
'here,' the fisherman whispers patiently on his bamboo
    platform, 'here,'
'here,' and they always see something else
and with those soaring butterfly vowels, oo and ee,
their mouths shape the name of the mountain that
    lives there,
appearing and disappearing like a moon or a sun.

4

There, etched in Yamanaka as an underwater fire,
in Baiu's silken rain, in summer's basket,
worn like a statue with its feet in the sea,
it blows at clouds and storms on the flute of its craters.
There, with the highest eye in its tower,
it is the first to see goraiko, the purple hole in the night,
the departure of the travelling sun, the stars' lofty
      rotation.
All of Japan dangles beneath it like a gondola of dreams
which it raises and cherishes and carries through the sky
beyond the reach of time.

friend

With the former glories run down, the idea
ripped apart in dreams and violated,
we dance past the fading frescoes,
never master or servant.

While you are alive I love you, as you write
I keep my eye on the registry of what we were,
a company of words and rhymes
in the city's open palace.

Today is later, a polluting summer,
and in this Theatre Today I look back and sketch
two croaking frogs, armed and
bent on the trough of farewell,
throats ragged from song,

but the slowest pages still blank.

Open Like a Shell,
Closed Like a Stone

1978

rolling stone

He began his life in the summer,
thoughts and memories.
Right there at the garden gate, he met a couple
with a scythe and a hat.

Dreams, stones rolling under his feet.

On his consuming swing
he waits for the night
when it will snow in the summer

and then it snows.
The black sun dispels the pale blue clouds,
the fathers leave their homes
to hunt for sons
the mothers murder their daughters
and lick the ash out of the fire
that must burn ever higher.

It has never been this wintry,
so say the sages.
The weasels and martens freeze in the fields,
the hawthorn blossoms,
the melting ships weave their sails
past towering roses.

How can he forget
the voluptuous fields
the frenzy of the moaning scythe
in the frozen hands
of the man with the hat
and the woman without eyes?

Love is death, cold
is summer, only he
is himself.

birthday

1

Naked on the rock she is a mystery to him
the way the peel on the plate is the fruit, yet not,
the way he keeps looking, yet doesn't see her,
two strangers who have known each other well,
cheating, robbing, consoling and cheating.

> *Does the sea wash the rocks?*
> *Or do the rocks wash the sea?*

2

She is a husk of flesh lying on a rock,
a butterfly with a butterfly circling round it,
and he is something that floats off and returns,
lies, wrecks and caresses, lies, floats off and returns.

Open like a shell,
closed like a stone.

3

They recognize each other in photos,
two tourists with rucksacks and sunglasses
hiking through each other's lives:
Dracula the beloved with his virginal nun.

> *But nobody died from the fangs.*
> *And nobody died from the light.*

4

And so another summer passes in the house of silence.
Heat, stones and stars mould their thoughts.
They calculate the season, their friends, the chances,
and talk about poems and money.

> *In the distance the sea sleeps on its chain,*
> *guarding the house.*

5

Now, more than ever, the hours count:
the blinded moth flies out of the shadow,
the lizard waits on the wall,
the snail eats the plant, the spider eats the fly,
the ants, the beetle,
the owl has turned to stone in its snow-white mask
and everyone waits,
everyone eats and waits, everyone waits
until the evening has passed like a life
and the night like a death

> *until life has passed like an evening*
> *and death has followed like night.*

nobody

More and more the invisible was named,
the blind man grew mightier.
How he wandered and called out to his echo!

which called back with the screech of gulls.
He is still searching among flags and vistas
for that same statue.

Sounds blow to the far side of the river.
Nobody is standing there.

Nothing takes shape. Newspapers melt,
photos fade. The stone is made of wax,
the notebook of ash, time takes itself
and repeats the appearance

until his life becomes a mirror
in which he disappears and appears,
but nobody looks at himself,
because nobody can see himself.

cries and whispers

1

Then came the inevitable day
when nobody listened
because nothing was said.

When he could sleep anywhere
with death in the room
and the cries and whispers
of dreams and diseases.

When he knew he had to preserve
his flesh as if in a tin
or the refrigerator. Preserving it
so that his eyes would stay clear
and with his eyes, himself,

whoever that might be.

2

One ear for whispered Swedish voices,
one eye for love in neglected parks,
for the track of the tear
on the cheek of the dead man,

who, through all those things, which
he had longed to say clearly,
so that they would become as clear as mirrors,
but which remained obscure,

those things determined him
and made him visible.
While eating slowly from the mirror,
he found himself

or who passed for him.

afternoon

Sometimes it doesn't take much.
An afternoon of burnished hours
that don't go together,
and him disbanded by himself,
sitting in various chairs,
but with a body or soul in each.

In a part of the room it is night.
Elsewhere, the past, holidays and war.
On the ceiling the sea touches the luminous beach,
and no hand guiding all this,
no ringmaster, no computer,
just him, that same self-same
someone, the disassembled
unreunited man,
in conversation with himself, dreaming and thinking,
present, invisible.

Someone who would eat and sleep later.
Someone with a watch and shoes.
Someone who left.
Someone who was going to leave.

Someone who would not go yet.

suitcase

Could you
fill these words
with sand?

Could you please
put the dream
in that box?

Would you
feed these lonely plates
with films, endless films,
in the shape of life?

Could you
turn silence into a hole
with room for us all,

would you
pay for my disappearance
with the money for a photo

until

not the glass but the shards
not the fabric but the tatters
not the unhealable whole
but the statue's missing hand,

until

I am allowed to become the suitcase
that tumbles like things.

hotels

Hotels! Always hotels
where their souls wandered,
lusting after their bodies.

Embracing each other over and over
devouring, consuming
in a thousand carnivorous beds,

encircled by the eyes
of guests and domestics
who recognized the fear.

The seasons called at the window,
imploring and vengeful,
shining and dancing,

as if in a real play,
in which she died, he died,

and they lay together under the spotlights,
two empty, gilded forms,

until her eyes smarted
from the glare on the marble,

until between the smells of roses
and expired banknotes

that same, numbing,
invariably identical night arrived

in which they celebrated their departure
and drank to their dishevelled,

decayed, distracted,
always lost

time.

last letter

In memory of Hans Andreus

On the white page
the name of the deceased
in his own hand.

Four letters, was that him?
All those words written,
all those poems of light,

and now nothing.

The bed is on the water,
the street is on the feet.
He has turned around
and gone back
where he came from.

tanners and leather-dyers, marrakesh

Like then and now, and then, and before
and then,
under the one hundred faces of time
and the one invisible face of God,
whose name I cannot say,
always the same,
it is me.
Within the walls of the city,
I slaughter, I tan, I dye
with my utterable name always forgotten,
with my visible
face always erased.
This is how I exist under the sun
in every level of hell,
in the stench of the hides, in the death of the knife,
in the stain of the dye,
making things.

the death of aegeus

You went to Crete
with the human sacrifice,
announcing yourself as Theseus,
son of Poseidon.
But no one saw you as
a child of the gods
until you killed the monster
in its labyrinth.

You came home
victorious.
But the evil fate
had already been written:
you failed to strike the black sails
that announced your death.

And so, with the dazzling white sails
forgotten in the hold
you sailed back in mourning,
drunk on wine and victory
and the bright sunlight
on the glittering sea.

Your father saw those baleful sails
and leapt into the wild water,
here, on Cape Sounion.

Now in this unthinkable later,
that same sea lies unmoved,
full of the fish-eaten burden
of the dead in its waves.

What happens every day then happens:
the sun paints it for the night
with blood, and then with gold,

and then comes the black
that always mourns.

homer on ithaca

The day is clear, the buzzard hovers over its prey.
A large box of silence
is being unpacked.

Over the sea's sparkling platter,
that other island floats.
The light is all porcelain,
a fragile vase around us.

Yesterday it happened again.
Today the hero goes to war.
Tomorrow he returns.

No, nothing has ever changed here.
Invisible beneath the olive, the blind man sleeps,
hiding the poet's secret in his eyes.

Sing in me, Muse!

those were the days

'I met you in the mountains.'
'I know you from the valley.'
'When people used to sing there.'
'A stream, with a linden.'
'On rainy days they always sang.'
'Red lips.'
'Mist or smoke from the factories.'
'Everyone has forgotten.'
'I still see it crystal clear before me.'
'In the old days, when . . .'
'Ah, painted over the photos . . .'
'The green of the hunter.'
'In cheerful colours . . .'
'The blue of the sea.'
'Those were the days.'

the thought

Time alone was not enough. It was
a different thought which, no matter how small,
how invisible like a bird that's too high,
circling overhead,
crushing the days to unnamed waiting,
unspeaking,
leaving only dust, grit, a dream
of something that would be

bitter if it were true, and because
it was true, bitterness hardened
the soft faces
in which they had been living.
Darker, harder
than you would expect from shadows,
the images crowded in,
making it clear

that no gleaming poem would be forged
from the fire no eye saved no face
visible

that what remained was a passing that faltered
when movement and the thought of movement fused

into death.

Present, Absent : 1970

poseidon and amphitrite,
villa stabia, pompeii

That infatuated moment
before heads turned into skulls
before death came to the gods

when they rode the sea on fiery steeds
and their lobster-hunting slaves
worked the tiled sails

and at the market I can only find
the fish
and not a trace of divinity

only the sea that ticks, sighs and splashes,
but lets the scent of mystery
dissipate

in a world that's grown as bare and lonely
as a dead gull on a rock

in time left as a beat
now that eternity has dwindled

the dark regularity of something small
without anything grand.

the green hunter

Look, there goes the green hunter,
the man you never see without a feather.
He doesn't have a feather now!
and he's hunting at night.

He hears what I hear,
memories, snippets from somewhere,
sounds that mean something,
ash from a fire.

Under the green trees
he follows the old words
and the words follow him, he tracks
and stalks and

the words imagine
women and hours,
just as dogs bark, the night is black,
and water, water.

Oh, thinks the green hunter under the trees,
you who I love, if I exist, seek me
and I'll seek you. I seek you, do you seek me?
I am here and will wait among carp and nests
full of eggs. I am not wearing a feather today but you must
recognize me. I will wait in my den,
which I cannot see.

t.

There is so little of you left
now you've been cremated,
a handful of ash that looks like ash,
and just last year you wanted me to kiss you.

athena,
on an amphora painted by psiax (brescia)

The unwise owl on your shield looks like a pigeon!
Between the dark animals and the ornamentation,
you stretch your hand out to the fight no one
can see.
Beside the straight folds of your peplos
the lance rises slowly like a phallus—
it's you, the better half of Pallas!

Now evening falls in the morning, night in the afternoon.
Heracles kills the lion, Heracles is given a drink,
Heracles wears the mask.
And you who protected him, with your face like a
    figurehead's!

Connections everywhere, interwoven threads!
I hear you in the crickets on Hydra,
I see you in the mirror of the galini,
under the pale Peloponnesus, on the opposite shore
when peace reigns—
and feel again the chill of the years that have disappeared,
the chill of your name, your helmet, my youth
and your eternal reserve—

and my time ends like Satyricon:
a weathered fresco on a deserted, overgrown hill,
the instruments broken or silenced,
and no one to measure how slowly the colours fade.

nothing at all

Life,
something you should be able to
remember
like a trip abroad,

discussing it afterwards
with male and female friends,
saying,

it really wasn't that bad,
life,
and seeing flashes of women, secrets
and landscapes

before leaning back in satisfaction,
but the dead can't lean back,

they can't do anything at all.

Closed Poems : 1964

a rainy part of the country

A rainy part of the country,
a rusty sword. An exhausted myth.
The immortals are dead and forgotten,
their home, a grave.
Their eye is a stone with which they see everything:

this point and its distance,
and all the lengths of time between—
the lust that encloses their bodies more and more
in a corrupt movement.

golden fiction

Look! They're opening up the fires.
The heathens fight for a handful of ash.
Tomorrow I leave again on my ship.

My friends are buried.
Under the trees their bodies continue.
Their souls are thousands of leaves
in the wind.

I hang my head in the gusts
and wonder. Why am I so sad
if my expectation goes no further than looking at fires
and a ship that is sailing?

The fraud sits in his room and writes it down.
Which lives give rise to his words? Which era?
Will real life ever reach him
and carry him off?

No, it will never carry him off.
The fraud sits in his room and writes
what the voices tell him.

The Black Poem ⋮ 1960

jungle

It's a thousand miles from here
a hole dug in the world
for nobody, and nobody
has ever been there.

The leaves cut and burn
a swirling vortex of animals
hunts in the canopy
invisible life cackles here below
the clearings drip with grease
from the moon.

The hissing river slides out of its dark den
and we dance in this racing tunnel of summer
to the ricochet of stone on stone
to the breath of our bodies blown through rock.

Our sweet and frightened flesh dances
the ghosts that eat people keep their distance
the ghosts that steal the pretty white thoughts
from the heads of the sleeping.

Low and orange the fires burn
I dance and dance
but I have never danced longer than my body
the night will never be as velvet soft as I thought.

m'hamid, tagounite

This is an incredible life
the doctor, the plantation owner,
the colonel—sunglasses, cane, leather gloves—
standing next to each other in Lili's bar
and drinking away the burning hours.

Outside the sun is punishing
soon the CTM bus will return
from the souk in Tagounite.

The biting sand blows in
and crunches in the beer
Berber soldiers in jeeps drive
on their endless playground.

The caid's wife wears a veil
the caid drinks tea on his divan
with pictures of Muhammad the Fifth
on the plastered wall.

Slowly the afternoon draws on
sand creeps and torments, creeps and torments,
the bus drives off to the black plain
and the mountains beyond.

The doctor, the plantation owner, the colonel
are left behind
in their own Sahara
going to bed at night behind bleeding walls.

Outside the cold and bitter moon

hunts lonely caravans
the soldiers of the guard
freeze in the Assyrian silence.

calera y chozas

The afternoon is a long fire
hung over an endless expanse of brown.

Calera y Chozas
expired farmers sleep in their beds
with gaping mouths the sound
of the afternoon slinks between the sickly houses.
at the end of the landscape
the mountains bare their teeth.

It never rains here
filthy dogs whimper
scratch and turn
in the dust.

No one gets on
the old man on the bench
leers at the life on the train
with avaricious eyes

it must be like this every day
the stationmaster rings the bell three times
and waves his red flag
the train shudders and shrieks
in the languishing landscape,

why would I ever come back
to Calera y Chozas?

Notes

Light Everywhere

pp. 3–26 LIGHT EVERYWHERE

A volume of poems by Cees Nooteboom, with etchings by Hugo Claus, published in December 2007 in an edition of 54 by Ergo Pers, Ghent, in collaboration with the antiquarian bookshop De Slegte, Antwerp. The volume included 12 poems ('The Candle', 'Full Moon', 'Kozan-Ji, Myoe Meditating', 'Exile', 'Purgatory', 'The Figure', 'Penobscot', 'Night', 'Glove, Year, Photo', 'Evening', 'Utopia Triumphans' and 'April auf dem Lande') and four ink drawings by Hugo Claus. (In the present volume, 'Evening' is about Claus' illness and is dedicated to his memory.) For the bibliophile edition, the drawings were etched on plates by Henri Hemelsoet. In 2008, De Slegte released a commercial edition as the sixth in a series of volumes on poetry.

p. 7 'Penobscot'

A bay near Castine in Maine, where Mary McCarthy spent her summers in the years before her death.

p. 9 'Exile'

Chong Er was later Duke Wen of Jin (697–628 BC).

pp.12–13 'Kozan-ji, Myoe Meditating'

Founded by Myoe (1173–1231), a learned Singon Buddhist monk. Kozan-ji is a small temple deep in the hills outside Kyoto. Nooteboom has visited this oasis of tranquility many times. A portrait of Myoe hangs in the temple.

p. 15 'The Candle'

Inspired by a photograph in Ricard Terré's 1957 series 'Setmana Santa', which appeared in *Temps de Silenci, Panorama de la fotografia espanyola dels anys 50 i 60* (Barcelona: Generalitat de Catalunya, 1992).

p. 16 'Purgatory'

Inspired by the fresco *La Divina Commedia di Dante* (The Divine Comedy by Dante, 1465) by Domenico di Michelino (1417–91) in Santa Maria del Fiore, Florence.

p. 20 'Glove, Year, Photo'

Based on *Half-Concealed Face*, a fashion photo by Nicolet, 1934 (The Hulton Getty Picture Collection, 1930s).

pp. 27–34 'A Trail in White Sand'

Written to works by Dutch painter, sculptor and graphic artist Cees Andriessen. The Sanskrit word *upanishad* comes from the verb *sad*, to sit, with *upa*, related to Latin *sub*, under, and *ni*, down. The meaning may be reduced to sitting down at the feet of, listening to, opening oneself to, in this case the lost voices of the Crutched Friars of the former cloister of Bentlage, and the sounds and images of the woods and fields round that old cloister which still partly stands and where the Cees Andriessen exhibition was held. The quote in the poem is from *The Upanishads*, Part 4 (Juan Mascaró trans., New York: Penguin Classics, 1965, p. 63): 'Like a flame without smoke, the size of a thumb, is the soul, the Lord of the past and the future, the same both today and tomorrow: This in Truth is That.'

pp. 35–49 ENCOUNTERS

On 15 February 2001, Jo Peters asked Cees Nooteboom to write a number of poems for the Zwarte Reeks (Black Series) published by Uitgeverij Herik, Landgraaf, and to invite an artist to illustrate the volume. Nooteboom suggested using Simone Sassen's photography. In June, when serious illness forced Peters to stop work, Frans Budé took over and requested the poet and the photographer to continue their work on *Encounters,* in collaboration with designer Piet Gerards. Peters died on 5 August 2001. The volume appeared in December 2001, as homage to the publisher. Thanks also to Ontwerpbureau Piet Gerards, Heerlen/Amsterdam, Drukkerij Econoom BV of Beek and Boekbinderij Martin van den Berg, Simpelveld, in collaboration with Jo Linssen, Landgraaf, all of whom charged no fee for their contributions; special thanks to De Kunstgunner of Hilversum, Tine Ruyters of Maastricht and the Stichting Brand Cultuurfonds Limburg.

p. 37 'Hesiod'

The epigraph is from Hesiod's *Fragments of Unknown Position*: 'with the pitiless smoke of pitch and cedarwood'.

Bittersweet

p. 61 'Paula Modersohn-Becker, Still Life, 1905'

Nooteboom saw Paula Modersohn-Becker's paintings in the Paula Modersohn-Becker Museum, Bremen.

p. 63 'The Poet Li Ho Finds an Arrow on the Battlefield'

Inspired by A. C. Graham's translation of Li Ho (791–817), a Chinese poet of the late T'ang period, in *Poems of the Late T'ang* (New York: Penguin, 1965).

p. 66 'Rilke, Painted by Paula Modersohn-Becker, 1906'

See note for p. 61.

p. 68 'The First Photo of God'

Inspired by a photograph by Eddy Posthuma de Boer.

p. 69 'Solanum Dulcamara'

Botanical name of bittersweet, a poisonous plant of the nightshade family.

p. 71 'Noche transfigurada'

Spanish for *Verklärte Nacht* (Schönberg).

Eye Sight

pp. 81–4 'Bashō'

Written as a response to both Bashō's (1644–94) work and a number of Sjoerd Bakker etchings and watercolours on the life and work of the great Japanese poet, commissioned by the literature department of the University of Amsterdam (where they, and the poems, are on permanent display). The lines in italics are quotes from Bashō's *Records of a Weather-Exposed Skeleton*, based here on the Dutch translation by Robert Hartzema, *Basho. Reisverslag van een verweerd skelet* (Amsterdam: Uitgeverij Karnak, 1979). Sorën is Russia and seventeen is the number of syllables in a haiku.

pp. 85–90 THE POET AND THINGS

Based on a reading of Lucretius' *De Rerum Natura*. Each poem relates to a specific passage. The Latin is drawn from the Loeb Classical Library edition (ed. Martin Ferguson Smith, 1975) and the English translations from *On the Nature of Things* (Martin Ferguson Smith trans., Indianapolis, IN: Hackett Publishing Company, 2001).

p. 85 'Lucretius'

Quin etiam refert nostris in versibus ipsis / cum quibus et quali sint ordine quaeque locata (Why, even in these verses of mine it is important in what groupings and order all the letters are placed), *De Rerum Natura*, II, 1013, 1014. Regarding the allusion to Cicero in 'Lucretius', I quote from P. H. Schrijvers, introduction to Lucretius, *Over de natuur* (Aeg. W. Timmerman trans., P. H. Schrijvers ed. and introd.; Ambo/Baarn: Athenaeum-Polak & Van Gennep, 1984), p. 20: 'In his critique of the Epicurean dogma that the world is the coincidental result of atomic collisions, Cicero seems to profit from the opportunities this traditional atomistic analogy offered him. He remarks that those who believe in the world arising coincidentally from atoms might just as well believe that, if countless figures shaped like the twenty-one letters of the Latin alphabet were thrown onto a heap, the letters shaken out on the ground could form the poetry of the Roman poet Ennius. Chance, according to Cicero, couldn't give rise to single line of poetry.'

p. 86 'Duality'

Huc accedit uti videamus, corpus ut ipsum | suscipere inmanis morbos durumque dolorem, | sic animum curas acris luctumque metumque; | quare participem leti quoque convenit esse. | Quin etiam morbis in corporis avius errat | saepe animus (There is the further point that, just as the body suffers dreadful diseases and pitiless pain, so the mind manifestly experiences the gripe of cares, grief, and fear, so the natural inference is that it has an equal share in death. Even during the body's sicknesses the mind often wanders from the path of reason), *De Rerum Natura*, III, 459–64.

p. 87 'Fire'

Donec flammai fulserunt flore coorto (until they burst into a flashing flower of flame), *De Rerum Natura*, I, 900.

p. 88 'Atoms'

Omnia cum rerum primordia sint in motu, | summa tamen summa videatur stare quiete (despite the movement of the primary elements of things, their entirety seems to stand entirely still), *De Rerum Natura,* II, 309, 310.

p. 89 'Mirror, Reflect'

Sunt igitur tenues formae rerum similesque | effigiae, singillatim quas cernere nemo | cum possit, tamen adsiduo crebroque repulsu | reiectae reddunt speculorum ex aequore visum (There are therefore fine forms and semblances of things which, though no one can perceive them individually, are constantly and rapidly repelled and rejected by the smooth reflecting surfaces and so produce a visible image), *De Rerum Natura*, IV, 104–8.

p. 90 'Justice Culinaire'

Quaeritur in primis quare, quod cuique libido / venerit, extemplo mens cogitet eius id ipsum (First of all we must ask how it is that the mind can instantly think of anything it wants), *De Rerum Natura*, IV, 779, 780.

pp. 92–113 EYE SIGHT

Published in January 1989 as a separate collection in a bibliophile edition of 190 copies, with colour reproductions of the work of Miguel Ybañez.

The quote from Guillermo Carnero, 'Variaciones y figuras sobre un tema de La Bruyère' (Variations and Figures on a Theme of La Bruyère) may be translated as follows: 'and by then the gong of your vocabulary had already dimmed your eyes', *Ensayo de una teoría de la visión* (Testing a Vision Theory) (Madrid: Poesia Hiperión, 1983).

pp. 92–9 'The Deception of Seeing'

The quote from Serafin Senosiáin, 'Mallarmé', may be translated as follows: 'They melt, the sound from the darkness that grows higher and higher until it almost cuts your throat, the body of the one passing through the temple, stared at by silence, consumed by light, the eye that pierces the windows in an unbearable longing to lose itself in the eye that pierces the windows in return with that same look', *El Espejo Invisible* (The Invisible Mirror) (Madrid: Libros Hiperión, 1984).

pp. 107–13 'The Litany of the Eye'

The quote from Serafin Senosiáin, 'Ibn Arabi', may be translated as follows: 'The litany of Ibn Arabi in his letter from Mecca takes your breath away. Abd Allah b. al-Arabi "dedicated himself to ascetic struggle and remained in desolate regions"; Muhammad b. Asraf "the man from Ronda", "wandered continually through mountains and wilderness, far from the world and without any fixed abode, and that for approximately thirty years", Salih al-Jarraz "went from Seville to the area around Ronda to live in the country, in isolation and away from other people"; Abd-al-Sallam, "the wanderer, travelled constantly through the mountains as a pilgrim, without ever settling in one place"; Abu Yahya al-Sinhayi "always travelled the beaches, preferring abandoned and isolated regions"; Ibn Arabi: "I said goodbye to the world to live in graveyards in solitude." The list evokes an intense longing for solitude, concentrating it, making it almost invisible in the burning eye of the Sufi. The shimmering leads the eye from the desert to light, from desolation to heat, from the silence containing the wind to the silence in which you can hear the stones', *El Espejo Invisible* (The Invisible Mirror) (Madrid: Libros Hiperión, 1984).

TRANSLATOR'S ACKNOWLEDGEMENTS

I thank Cees Nooteboom for taking the time to read these translations and acknowledge his suggestions and corrections. In some cases the translated versions deviate from the originals at the poet's request.

David Colmer
Amsterdam, 2013